Introduction

"The Grilling Handbook" is your ultimate guide to mastering the art of grilling. Packed with expert tips, techniques, and mouthwatering recipes, this comprehensive cookbook is a go-to resource for anyone looking to take their grilling skills to the next level.

Within the pages of "The Grilling Handbook," you'll find a wealth of knowledge that will empower you to become a true grilling aficionado. Whether you're a seasoned grill master or a beginner, this cookbook caters to all levels of expertise, providing step-by-step instructions and detailed explanations of grilling fundamentals.

Discover the secrets of achieving the perfect sear, creating flavorful marinades and rubs, and mastering the art of indirect grilling. From juicy steaks and tender ribs to succulent seafood and vibrant grilled vegetables, the cookbook presents a diverse range of recipes that celebrate the versatility of the grill.

"The Grilling Handbook" goes beyond just recipes, delving into the science behind grilling and offering insights into different grilling techniques, such as direct heat, indirect heat, and smoking. Learn about the best cuts of meat for grilling, the importance of temperature control, and how to properly use various grilling tools and accessories.

Caprese Steak

Ingredients:

4 steak cuts of your choice (such as ribeye, sirloin, or filet mignon)
Salt and pepper, to taste
2 tablespoons olive oil
4 slices fresh mozzarella cheese
4 large tomato slices
1/4 cup fresh basil leaves
Balsamic glaze, for drizzling

Instructions:

Preheat your grill to medium-high heat.
Season the steak cuts with salt and pepper on both sides.
Drizzle olive oil over the steak cuts and rub it in to evenly coat them.
Place the seasoned steak cuts on the preheated grill and cook to your desired level of doneness, usually about 4-5 minutes per side for medium-rare, depending on the thickness of the steak. Adjust the cooking time based on your preference.
In the last few minutes of grilling, top each steak with a slice of fresh mozzarella cheese and allow it to melt slightly.
Remove the steak cuts from the grill and transfer them to a serving platter or individual plates.
Top each steak with a slice of tomato and a few fresh basil leaves.
Drizzle the Caprese steaks with balsamic glaze, which adds a tangy and sweet flavor.
Serve the Caprese Steak immediately while it's still warm and the cheese is melted. You can serve it with a side of roasted vegetables, a fresh salad, or some crusty bread.
Caprese Steak combines the rich and juicy flavors of grilled steak with the freshness of tomatoes, basil, and mozzarella. The balsamic glaze adds a delightful touch of sweetness and acidity. It's a mouthwatering dish that is perfect for summer grilling or any occasion where you want to impress your guests with a flavorful and elegant steak preparation. Enjoy!

Grilled Guacamole

Ingredients:

3 ripe avocados
1 lime, juiced
1/4 cup red onion, finely chopped
1/4 cup fresh cilantro, chopped
1 jalapeño pepper, seeded and finely chopped
2 Roma tomatoes, seeded and diced
2 cloves garlic, minced
Salt and pepper, to taste
Olive oil, for grilling
Tortilla chips, for serving

Instructions:

Preheat your grill to medium-high heat.

Cut the avocados in half lengthwise and remove the pits. Brush the avocado halves lightly with olive oil to prevent sticking to the grill.
Place the avocado halves face-down on the preheated grill and cook for about 2-3 minutes, or until grill marks appear. Remove from the grill and let them cool slightly.
Scoop out the grilled avocado flesh into a medium bowl. Mash the avocado with a fork until desired texture is reached (smooth or chunky).
Add the lime juice, red onion, cilantro, jalapeño pepper, diced tomatoes, and minced garlic to the bowl with the mashed avocado. Mix well to combine.
Season the grilled guacamole with salt and pepper to taste. Adjust the seasonings according to your preference.

Serve the Grilled Guacamole immediately with tortilla chips or as a condiment for tacos, grilled meats, or sandwiches.
Grilling the avocados adds a smoky flavor and enhances the creaminess of the guacamole. The combination of grilled avocado, fresh vegetables, and zesty lime juice creates a unique and delicious twist on the classic guacamole recipe. It's a fantastic appetizer or side dish that will surely impress your guests at any gathering or barbecue. Enjoy!

Mediterranean Salmon Skewers

Ingredients:

1 lb salmon fillet, cut into 1-inch cubes
1 red onion, cut into 1-inch pieces
1 red bell pepper, cut into 1-inch pieces
1 yellow bell pepper, cut into 1-inch pieces
1/4 cup olive oil
2 tablespoons lemon juice
2 cloves garlic, minced
1 teaspoon dried oregano
1 teaspoon dried thyme
1 teaspoon ground cumin
Salt and black pepper, to taste
Wooden skewers

Instructions:

Preheat your grill to medium-high heat.
Soak wooden skewers in water for at least 20 minutes before grilling.
In a small bowl, whisk together the olive oil, lemon juice, minced garlic, dried oregano, dried thyme, ground cumin, salt, and black pepper.
Thread the salmon cubes, red onion, and bell peppers onto the skewers, alternating between each.
Brush the marinade generously over the skewers, making sure all sides are coated.
Place the skewers on the grill and cook for about 6-8 minutes, turning once halfway through, or until the salmon is cooked through.
Once the skewers are cooked, remove them from the grill and let them rest for a few minutes.
Serve the Mediterranean salmon skewers hot with your favorite sides.
Enjoy your delicious Mediterranean Salmon Skewers!

Grilled Ranch Potatoes

Ingredients:

4-5 medium-sized potatoes, washed and sliced into 1/4 inch rounds
2 tablespoons olive oil
1 packet (1 oz) ranch dressing mix
Salt and pepper, to taste
Chopped fresh parsley or chives, for garnish

Instructions:

Preheat your grill to medium-high heat.
In a large bowl, toss the potato slices with olive oil, ranch dressing mix, salt, and pepper until evenly coated.
Place the potato slices on the grill and cook for about 8-10 minutes on each side or until the potatoes are tender and browned.
Remove the potatoes from the grill and transfer to a serving dish.
Garnish with chopped fresh parsley or chives.
Serve hot as a side dish to your favorite grilled meat or fish.
Enjoy your delicious Grilled Ranch Potatoes!

Grilled Cod Tacos with Chipotle Crema

Ingredients:

1 lb. cod fillets
2 tbsp. olive oil
1 tbsp. chili powder
1 tsp. cumin
1/2 tsp. garlic powder
Salt and pepper
8 corn tortillas
1 cup shredded cabbage
1 avocado, sliced
1 lime, cut into wedges

For the chipotle crema:

1/2 cup sour cream
1 tbsp. adobo sauce (from a can of chipotle peppers)
Juice of 1/2 lime
Salt to taste

Instructions:

Preheat grill to medium-high heat.
In a small bowl, mix together olive oil, chili powder, cumin, garlic powder, salt, and pepper.
Brush both sides of the cod fillets with the spice mixture.
Grill the cod for about 3-4 minutes per side, or until cooked through.
While the cod is grilling, make the chipotle crema. In a small bowl, mix together sour cream, adobo sauce, lime juice, and salt. Adjust seasoning to taste.
Warm the corn tortillas on the grill or in a skillet.
Assemble the tacos by placing some shredded cabbage on each tortilla, followed by a piece of grilled cod, sliced avocado, and a dollop of chipotle crema. Serve with lime wedges on the side.
Enjoy your delicious Grilled Cod Tacos with Chipotle Crema!

Kalbi (Korean Short Ribs)

Ingredients:

3 lbs. Korean-style short ribs (flanken cut)
1/2 cup soy sauce
1/2 cup brown sugar
1/4 cup rice wine or sake
1/4 cup sesame oil
1/4 cup chopped green onions
6 cloves garlic, minced
1 tbsp. grated ginger
1/2 tsp. black pepper

Instructions:

In a large bowl, whisk together soy sauce, brown sugar, rice wine or sake, sesame oil, green onions, garlic, ginger, and black pepper.
Add the short ribs to the marinade and toss to coat. Cover and refrigerate for at least 2 hours, or overnight.
Preheat grill to medium-high heat.
Remove the short ribs from the marinade and shake off any excess.
Grill the short ribs for about 3-4 minutes per side, or until cooked to your liking.
Serve the kalbi hot off the grill with steamed rice, kimchi, and other Korean side dishes.
Enjoy your delicious Korean-style Kalbi (Short Ribs) with your family and friends!

Balsamic Grilled Mushrooms

Ingredients:

1 pound of fresh mushrooms, cleaned and stems removed
2 tablespoons olive oil
2 tablespoons balsamic vinegar
2 cloves garlic, minced
1 tablespoon fresh thyme leaves
Salt and pepper, to taste
Chopped fresh parsley, for garnish

Instructions:

Preheat your grill to medium-high heat.
In a small bowl, whisk together olive oil, balsamic vinegar, garlic, thyme, salt, and pepper.
Brush the mushroom caps generously with the olive oil mixture.
Place the mushroom caps on the grill and cook for about 5-6 minutes on each side or until the mushrooms are tender and slightly charred.
Remove the mushrooms from the grill and transfer to a serving dish.
Garnish with chopped fresh parsley.
Serve hot as a side dish to your favorite grilled meat or fish.
Enjoy your delicious Balsamic Grilled Mushrooms!

Grilled Chicken Quesadillas

Ingredients:

2 boneless, skinless chicken breasts
1 teaspoon ground cumin
1 teaspoon chili powder
1/2 teaspoon garlic powder
Salt and pepper, to taste
4 large flour tortillas
2 cups shredded cheese (cheddar, Monterey Jack, or a combination)
1/2 cup diced tomatoes
1/4 cup diced red onion
1/4 cup chopped fresh cilantro
Sour cream and salsa, for serving

Instructions:

Preheat your grill to medium-high heat.
Season the chicken breasts with cumin, chili powder, garlic powder, salt, and pepper. Grill the chicken for 6-8 minutes per side or until cooked through. Let the chicken rest for 5 minutes before slicing it into thin strips.
Place one tortilla on a flat surface and sprinkle 1/2 cup of shredded cheese over half of the tortilla.
Add 1/4 cup of diced tomatoes, 2 tablespoons of diced red onion, and 1 tablespoon of chopped cilantro on top of the cheese.
Add a layer of sliced chicken on top of the vegetables.
Fold the tortilla in half over the filling.
Repeat steps 3-6 with the remaining tortillas and filling ingredients.
Place the quesadillas on the grill and cook for 2-3 minutes per side, or until the cheese is melted and the tortilla is crispy.
Serve the quesadillas with sour cream and salsa on the side.
Enjoy your delicious Grilled Chicken Quesadillas!

Grilled Hanger Steak

Ingredients:

1 pound hanger steak
2 tablespoons olive oil
2 cloves garlic, minced
2 teaspoons dried oregano
1 teaspoon smoked paprika
1 teaspoon salt
1/2 teaspoon black pepper

Instructions:

Remove the hanger steak from the fridge and let it come to room temperature for about 30 minutes.
Preheat the grill to medium-high heat.
In a small bowl, mix together the olive oil, minced garlic, dried oregano, smoked paprika, salt, and black pepper.
Brush the mixture onto both sides of the hanger steak.
Place the steak on the grill and cook for about 3-4 minutes per side, or until the internal temperature reaches 135°F for medium-rare.
Once the steak is cooked, remove it from the grill and let it rest for about 5 minutes to allow the juices to redistribute.
Slice the steak against the grain into thin strips and serve with your favorite sides.
Enjoy your delicious Grilled Hanger Steak!

Grilled Zucchini

Ingredients:

2-3 medium-sized zucchini, washed and sliced lengthwise into 1/4 inch strips
2 tablespoons olive oil
1 tablespoon balsamic vinegar
2 cloves garlic, minced
1 teaspoon dried oregano
Salt and pepper, to taste
Chopped fresh parsley, for garnish

Instructions:

Preheat your grill to medium-high heat.
In a small bowl, whisk together olive oil, balsamic vinegar, garlic, oregano, salt, and pepper.
Brush the zucchini slices generously with the olive oil mixture.
Place the zucchini slices on the grill and cook for about 3-4 minutes on each side or until the zucchini is tender and charred.
Remove the zucchini from the grill and transfer to a serving dish.
Garnish with chopped fresh parsley.
Serve hot as a side dish to your favorite grilled meat or fish.
Enjoy your delicious Grilled ucchini!

Grilled Tilapia

Ingredients:

4 tilapia fillets, about 6 oz each
2 tablespoons olive oil
2 tablespoons fresh lime juice
1 teaspoon ground cumin
1 teaspoon chili powder
1/2 teaspoon garlic powder
Salt and pepper, to taste
Lime wedges, for garnish

Instructions:

Preheat your grill to medium-high heat.
In a small bowl, whisk together olive oil, lime juice, cumin, chili powder, garlic powder, salt, and pepper.
Brush the tilapia fillets generously with the olive oil mixture.
Place the tilapia fillets on the grill and cook for about 4-5 minutes on each side or until the tilapia is cooked through and flakes easily with a fork.
Remove the tilapia from the grill and transfer to a serving plate.
Garnish with lime wedges.
Serve hot with a side of grilled vegetables or a fresh salad.
Enjoy your delicious Grilled Tilapia!

Grilled Fish

Ingredients:

4 fish fillets, about 6 oz each (you can use any white fish like tilapia, cod, or haddock)
2 tablespoons olive oil
1 tablespoon lemon juice
2 teaspoons paprika
2 teaspoons garlic powder
1 teaspoon onion powder
Salt and pepper, to taste
Lemon wedges, for garnish

Instructions:

Preheat your grill to medium-high heat.
In a small bowl, whisk together olive oil, lemon juice, paprika, garlic powder, onion powder, salt, and pepper.
Brush the fish fillets generously with the olive oil mixture.
Place the fish fillets on the grill and cook for about 4-5 minutes on each side or until the fish is cooked through and flakes easily with a fork.
Remove the fish from the grill and transfer to a serving plate.
Garnish with lemon wedges.
Serve hot with a side of grilled vegetables or a fresh salad.
Enjoy your delicious Grilled Fish!

Grilled Halibut

Ingredients:

4 halibut fillets, about 6 oz each
2 tablespoons olive oil
1 tablespoon lemon juice
2 teaspoons dried oregano
2 teaspoons garlic powder
1 teaspoon onion powder
Salt and pepper, to taste
Lemon wedges, for garnish

Instructions:

Preheat your grill to medium-high heat.
In a small bowl, whisk together olive oil, lemon juice, dried oregano, garlic powder, onion powder, salt, and pepper.
Brush the halibut fillets generously with the olive oil mixture.
Place the halibut fillets on the grill and cook for about 4-5 minutes on each side or until the halibut is cooked through and flakes easily with a fork.
Remove the halibut from the grill and transfer to a serving plate.
Garnish with lemon wedges.
Serve hot with a side of grilled vegetables or a fresh salad.
Enjoy your delicious Grilled Halibut!

Asian BBQ Salmon

Ingredients:

4 salmon fillets, about 6 oz each
1/4 cup soy sauce
1/4 cup brown sugar
1/4 cup honey
2 tablespoons rice vinegar
2 tablespoons sesame oil
1 tablespoon minced garlic
1 tablespoon grated ginger
1 tablespoon sriracha sauce (optional)
2 green onions, thinly sliced
Sesame seeds, for garnish
Salt and pepper, to taste

Instructions:

Preheat your grill to medium-high heat.
In a small bowl, whisk together soy sauce, brown sugar, honey, rice vinegar, sesame oil, minced garlic, grated ginger, and sriracha sauce (if using).
Season salmon fillets with salt and pepper, then brush generously with the soy sauce mixture.
Place the salmon fillets skin-side down on the grill and cook for about 5-6 minutes.
Flip the salmon fillets and brush again with the soy sauce mixture. Cook for an additional 4-5 minutes or until the salmon is cooked to your desired level of doneness.
Remove the salmon from the grill and transfer to a serving plate.
Garnish with thinly sliced green onions and sesame seeds.
Serve hot with steamed rice and stir-fried vegetables.
Enjoy your delicious Asian BBQ Salmon!

Grilled Pineapple Chicken

Ingredients:

4 boneless, skinless chicken breasts
2 cups fresh pineapple chunks
1/4 cup olive oil
1/4 cup soy sauce
2 tablespoons honey
2 tablespoons apple cider vinegar
2 cloves garlic, minced
1/2 teaspoon ground ginger
1/4 teaspoon black pepper
Bamboo skewers, soaked in water for 30 minutes

Instructions:

Preheat your grill or grill pan to medium-high heat.
In a small bowl, whisk together the olive oil, soy sauce, honey, apple cider vinegar, minced garlic, ground ginger, and black pepper.
Cut the chicken breasts into 1-inch pieces and add them to the bowl, tossing to coat them with the marinade.
Thread the chicken and pineapple chunks onto the bamboo skewers, alternating between the two.
Grill the chicken skewers for 5-6 minutes per side, or until the chicken is cooked through and the pineapple is lightly charred.
Serve the grilled pineapple chicken hot, garnished with chopped fresh herbs, if desired. You can also serve them with a side of your choice, such as rice, quinoa, or a salad.
Enjoy your delicious and flavorful Grilled Pineapple Chicken!

Spicy Grilled Shrimp

Ingredients:

1 lb large shrimp, peeled and deveined
1/4 cup olive oil
2 tablespoons lime juice
2 cloves garlic, minced
1 teaspoon smoked paprika
1/2 teaspoon cumin powder
1/2 teaspoon chili powder
1/4 teaspoon cayenne pepper
Salt and black pepper, to taste
Bamboo skewers, soaked in water for 30 minutes

Instructions:

Preheat your grill or grill pan to medium-high heat.
In a small bowl, whisk together the olive oil, lime juice, minced garlic, smoked paprika, cumin powder, chili powder, cayenne pepper, salt, and black pepper.
Add the shrimp to the bowl and toss to coat them with the marinade.
Thread the shrimp onto the bamboo skewers, making sure they are evenly spaced.
Grill the shrimp skewers for 2-3 minutes per side or until they are pink and lightly charred.
Serve the spicy grilled shrimp hot, garnished with chopped fresh herbs, if desired. You can also serve them with a side of your choice, such as rice, quinoa, or a salad.
Enjoy your delicious and spicy grilled shrimp!

Beer Can Burgers

Ingredients:

2 lbs. ground beef
1/2 cup breadcrumbs
2 eggs
2 tbsp. Worcestershire sauce
1 tbsp. garlic powder
1 tbsp. onion powder
1 tsp. salt
1/2 tsp. black pepper
6 slices bacon
6 slices cheddar cheese
1/2 cup BBQ sauce
6 hamburger buns
6 empty beer cans
Olive oil

Instructions:

Preheat grill to medium-high heat.
In a large bowl, mix together ground beef, breadcrumbs, eggs, Worcestershire sauce, garlic powder, onion powder, salt, and pepper until well combined.
Divide the beef mixture into 6 portions and shape each portion around a beer can, making a well in the center.
Wrap each burger in a slice of bacon and brush with olive oil.
Place the burgers on the grill, with the beer cans facing down, and cook for 10-12 minutes.
Carefully remove the beer cans from the burgers and fill the well with BBQ sauce.
Top each burger with a slice of cheddar cheese and cook for an additional 1-2 minutes, until cheese is melted.
Serve the burgers on hamburger buns with your favorite toppings.
Enjoy your Beer Can Burgers!

Grilled Red Snapper

Ingredients:

4 red snapper fillets, about 6 ounces each
2 tablespoons olive oil
1 tablespoon fresh lemon juice
2 garlic cloves, minced
1/2 teaspoon paprika
1/2 teaspoon cumin
1/2 teaspoon salt
1/4 teaspoon black pepper
Lemon wedges, for serving
Fresh parsley, chopped, for garnish

Instructions:

Preheat your grill to medium-high heat.
In a small bowl, whisk together the olive oil, lemon juice, minced garlic, paprika, cumin, salt, and black pepper.
Brush the snapper fillets with the marinade, making sure they are well coated.
Place the fillets on the grill, skin-side down.
Grill the fish for about 4-5 minutes on each side, or until the flesh is opaque and flakes easily with a fork.
Remove the fish from the grill and transfer them to a serving platter.
Garnish with chopped fresh parsley and serve hot, with lemon wedges on the side.
Enjoy your delicious and healthy Grilled Red Snapper!

Chicken Satay

Ingredients:

1 lb boneless, skinless chicken breasts or thighs, cut into thin strips
1/2 cup coconut milk
2 tablespoons soy sauce
2 tablespoons honey
1 tablespoon curry powder
1 tablespoon turmeric powder
1 tablespoon cumin powder
1 tablespoon coriander powder
1 teaspoon garlic powder
1 teaspoon ginger powder
1/2 teaspoon salt
1/4 teaspoon black pepper
Bamboo skewers, soaked in water for 30 minutes

Instructions:

In a large bowl, mix together the coconut milk, soy sauce, honey, curry powder, turmeric powder, cumin powder, coriander powder, garlic powder, ginger powder, salt, and black pepper.
Add the chicken strips to the bowl and toss to coat them with the marinade. Cover the bowl with plastic wrap and refrigerate for at least 2 hours, or overnight.
Preheat your grill or grill pan to medium-high heat.
Thread the chicken strips onto the bamboo skewers, making sure they are evenly spaced.
Grill the chicken skewers for 3-4 minutes per side or until cooked through.
Serve the chicken satay hot, garnished with chopped peanuts and fresh cilantro. You can also serve it with a side of peanut sauce for dipping.
Enjoy your delicious Chicken Satay!

Caprese Steak

Ingredients:

4 6-ounce beef sirloin steaks
1 tablespoon olive oil
Salt and black pepper, to taste
4 slices of fresh mozzarella cheese
4 slices of fresh tomato
1/4 cup chopped fresh basil leaves
Balsamic glaze, for serving

Instructions:

Preheat your grill or grill pan to medium-high heat.
Brush the steaks with olive oil and season them with salt and black pepper.
Grill the steaks for 4-5 minutes per side or until they are cooked to your desired level of doneness.
During the last 2 minutes of cooking, place a slice of mozzarella cheese and a slice of tomato on top of each steak.
Remove the steaks from the grill and let them rest for a few minutes.
Sprinkle the chopped basil leaves over the top of the steaks.
Drizzle the balsamic glaze over the top of each steak and serve hot.
Enjoy your delicious and flavorful Caprese Steak!

Grilled Ahi Tuna with Lemony Labneh

Ingredients:

4 6-ounce ahi tuna steaks
2 tablespoons olive oil
1/2 teaspoon salt
1/4 teaspoon black pepper
1 cup labneh or Greek yogurt
1 tablespoon fresh lemon juice
1 teaspoon lemon zest
2 cloves garlic, minced
2 tablespoons chopped fresh parsley

Instructions:

Preheat your grill to high heat.
Brush the ahi tuna steaks with olive oil and season them with salt and black pepper.
Grill the tuna steaks for 2-3 minutes per side, or until they are seared on the outside but still rare in the middle.
In a small bowl, whisk together the labneh or Greek yogurt, lemon juice, lemon zest, minced garlic, and chopped parsley.
Serve the grilled ahi tuna steaks hot, topped with a dollop of the lemony labneh sauce.
Enjoy your delicious and healthy Grilled Ahi Tuna with Lemony Labneh!

Veggie Kabobs

Ingredients:

1 red bell pepper, seeded and cut into 1-inch pieces
1 green bell pepper, seeded and cut into 1-inch pieces
1 yellow squash, cut into 1/2-inch slices
1 zucchini, cut into 1/2-inch slices
1 red onion, cut into 1-inch pieces
8-10 cherry tomatoes
1/4 cup olive oil
2 tablespoons balsamic vinegar
1 tablespoon honey
1 tablespoon Dijon mustard
1 teaspoon dried basil
1/2 teaspoon salt
1/4 teaspoon black pepper
Bamboo skewers, soaked in water for 30 minutes

Instructions:

Preheat your grill or grill pan to medium-high heat.
In a large bowl, whisk together the olive oil, balsamic vinegar, honey, Dijon mustard, dried basil, salt, and black pepper.
Add the chopped vegetables to the bowl and toss to coat them with the marinade.
Thread the vegetables onto the bamboo skewers, making sure they are evenly spaced.
Grill the vegetable kabobs for 3-4 minutes per side or until tender and lightly charred.
Serve the veggie kabobs hot, garnished with chopped fresh herbs or a sprinkle of grated Parmesan cheese, if desired.
Enjoy your delicious and healthy Veggie Kabobs!

Pineapple Bun Bacon Cheeseburger

Ingredients:

1 pound ground beef
4 slices of bacon
4 slices of cheddar cheese
4 pineapple buns
1/4 cup diced onion
1/4 cup diced pickles
2 tablespoons ketchup
2 tablespoons mayonnaise
1 tablespoon yellow mustard
1 teaspoon garlic powder
Salt and pepper, to taste

Instructions:

Preheat your grill or grill pan to medium-high heat.
Divide the ground beef into four equal portions and shape into patties. Season each patty with garlic powder, salt, and pepper.
Place the bacon on the grill and cook until crispy. Remove the bacon from the grill and set it aside.
Grill the beef patties for 3-4 minutes per side or until cooked to your desired level of doneness.
While the patties are cooking, mix together the ketchup, mayonnaise, and yellow mustard in a small bowl.
Toast the pineapple buns on the grill for 1-2 minutes until lightly browned.
Assemble the burgers: place a beef patty on the bottom half of each pineapple bun. Top each patty with a slice of cheddar cheese, a slice of bacon, and some diced onion and pickles.
Spread the ketchup-mayo-mustard sauce on the top half of each pineapple bun and place it on top of the burger.
Serve the burgers immediately, while still hot.
Enjoy your Pineapple Bun Bacon Cheeseburger!

Greek Salmon Burgers

Ingredients:

1 pound fresh salmon fillet, skin removed
1/4 cup panko breadcrumbs
1/4 cup crumbled feta cheese
1/4 cup chopped fresh parsley
2 tablespoons chopped fresh dill
1 egg, beaten
1 tablespoon lemon juice
1 garlic clove, minced
Salt and pepper to taste
4 hamburger buns
Lettuce, tomato, and red onion for toppings (optional)

Instructions:

Cut the salmon fillet into small pieces and place them in a food processor. Pulse until the salmon is finely chopped but not pureed.
In a large mixing bowl, combine the chopped salmon, panko breadcrumbs, crumbled feta cheese, chopped fresh parsley, chopped fresh dill, beaten egg, lemon juice, minced garlic, salt, and pepper. Mix well to combine.
Divide the mixture into 4 equal portions and shape them into patties.
Preheat your grill to medium-high heat.
Grill the salmon burgers for 3-4 minutes per side, or until they are cooked through.
During the last minute of cooking, toast the hamburger buns on the grill.
Assemble the burgers by placing a salmon patty on the bottom of each bun.
Add lettuce, tomato, and red onion on top of the salmon patty, if desired.
Serve hot and enjoy your delicious Greek salmon burgers!
Note: You can also serve these burgers with tzatziki sauce or a squeeze of lemon juice for extra flavor.

Grilled Shrimp Tacos with Sriracha Slaw

For the shrimp:

1 pound large shrimp, peeled and deveined
2 cloves garlic, minced
1 tablespoon olive oil
1 tablespoon lime juice
1 teaspoon chili powder
Salt and pepper to taste

For the sriracha slaw:

2 cups shredded cabbage
1/4 cup mayonnaise
2 tablespoons sriracha sauce
1 tablespoon lime juice
Salt and pepper to taste

For serving:

8 small corn tortillas
Lime wedges for serving
Chopped fresh cilantro for garnish

Instructions:

Preheat your grill to medium-high heat.
In a large mixing bowl, combine the shrimp, minced garlic, olive oil, lime juice, chili powder, salt, and pepper. Mix well to coat the shrimp evenly.
Grill the shrimp for 2-3 minutes per side, or until they are pink and cooked through.
In a separate mixing bowl, whisk together the mayonnaise, sriracha sauce, lime juice, salt, and pepper. Add the shredded cabbage and toss until well coated with the dressing.
Warm the corn tortillas on the grill for 30 seconds on each side.
To assemble the tacos, place a small amount of the sriracha slaw on each tortilla, followed by a few grilled shrimp.
Top with chopped fresh cilantro and serve with lime wedges on the side.
Enjoy your delicious grilled shrimp tacos with sriracha slaw!

Jalapeño Popper Burgers

Ingredients:

1 pound ground beef
1/2 cup panko breadcrumbs
1 egg
1/4 cup diced pickled jalapeños
1/4 cup cream cheese, softened
4 slices of cheddar cheese
4 hamburger buns
Lettuce, tomato, and onion for toppings (optional)

Instructions:

In a large mixing bowl, combine the ground beef, panko breadcrumbs, egg, and diced pickled jalapeños. Mix until well combined.
Divide the mixture into 4 equal portions and shape them into patties.
In a small bowl, mix together the softened cream cheese and diced pickled jalapeños until well combined.
Preheat your grill to medium-high heat.
Grill the burgers for 3-4 minutes per side, or until they are cooked to your desired level of doneness.
During the last minute of cooking, add a slice of cheddar cheese to each burger and allow it to melt.
Toast the hamburger buns on the grill for 30-60 seconds, or until lightly browned.
Spread the cream cheese mixture on the bottom of each bun.
Place a burger patty on top of the cream cheese mixture, and top with lettuce, tomato, and onion, if desired.
Serve hot and enjoy your delicious jalapeño popper burgers!
Note: If you prefer a milder flavor, you can use fresh jalapeños instead of pickled jalapeños. Simply roast them on the grill for a few minutes before chopping and adding them to the beef mixture.

California Grilled Chicken

Ingredients:

4 boneless, skinless chicken breasts
1 avocado, sliced
4 slices of bacon, cooked and crumbled
1 tomato, sliced
1/2 red onion, sliced
1/4 cup chopped fresh cilantro
2 tablespoons olive oil
2 tablespoons lime juice
1 teaspoon garlic powder
1 teaspoon smoked paprika
1/2 teaspoon salt
1/4 teaspoon black pepper

Instructions:

Preheat your grill or grill pan to medium-high heat.
In a small bowl, whisk together the olive oil, lime juice, garlic powder, smoked paprika, salt, and black pepper.
Place the chicken breasts in a large bowl and pour the marinade over them. Toss to coat the chicken evenly.
Grill the chicken breasts for 6-8 minutes per side, or until they are cooked through.
Assemble the California Grilled Chicken: Place each chicken breast on a plate and top with sliced avocado, crumbled bacon, sliced tomato, and sliced red onion. Garnish with chopped cilantro.
Serve the California Grilled Chicken hot, with a side of your choice, such as rice, qinoa, or a salad.
Enjoy your delicious and healthy California Grilled Chicken!

Grilled Asparagus

Ingredients:

1 pound fresh asparagus spears
2 tablespoons olive oil
2 cloves garlic, minced
Salt and pepper
Lemon wedges for serving (optional)

Instructions:

Preheat your grill to medium-high heat.
Wash the asparagus spears and snap off the tough, woody ends.
In a small bowl, whisk together the olive oil, minced garlic, salt, and pepper.
Toss the asparagus spears in the garlic oil mixture, making sure to coat them evenly.
Place the asparagus on the grill and cook for 4-6 minutes, turning occasionally, or until the asparagus is lightly charred and tender.
Remove the asparagus from the grill and serve hot with lemon wedges on the side, if desired.
Enjoy your delicious grilled asparagus as a healthy side dish!

Mexican Street Corn (Elote)

Ingredients:

4 ears of corn, husks removed
1/4 cup mayonnaise
1/4 cup sour cream
1/4 cup crumbled cotija cheese (or feta cheese)
1 teaspoon chili powder
1/4 teaspoon garlic powder
1/4 teaspoon smoked paprika
1/4 teaspoon salt
1/4 teaspoon black pepper
Lime wedges and chopped fresh cilantro for garnish

Instructions:

Preheat your grill to medium-high heat.
Grill the ears of corn, turning occasionally, until they are lightly charred on all sides, about 8-10 minutes.
naise, sour cream, cotija cheese, chili powder, garlic powder, smoked paprika, salt, and black pepper.
Once the corn is cooked, brush each ear with the mayo mixture, making sure to coat them evenly on all sides.
Sprinkle additional cotija cheese and chili powder on top of the corn.
Serve the corn with lime wedges and chopped fresh cilantro for garnish.
Enjoy your delicious Mexican street corn (elote) as a side dish or a snack!

Grilled Corn Salsa

Ingredients:

4 ears of corn, husks and silks removed
1 red bell pepper, seeded and chopped
1/2 red onion, chopped
1 jalapeno pepper, seeded and finely chopped
1/4 cup chopped fresh cilantro
2 tablespoons lime juice
2 tablespoons olive oil
Salt and pepper

Instructions:

Preheat your grill to medium-high heat.
Brush the ears of corn with olive oil and place them on the grill. Grill the corn, turning occasionally, until the kernels are lightly charred, about 8-10 minutes. Remove from the grill and let cool.
Once the corn has cooled, cut the kernels off the cob and place them in a large bowl. Add the chopped red bell pepper, red onion, jalapeno pepper, chopped cilantro, lime juice, and olive oil to the bowl. Toss to combine.
Season with salt and pepper to taste.
Let the salsa sit for at least 30 minutes before serving to allow the flavors to meld together.
Serve with tortilla chips, on top of grilled chicken or fish, or as a side dish.
Enjoy your delicious grilled corn salsa!

Grilled Pork Tenderloin

Ingredients:

1 pork tenderloin, about 1 1/2 pounds
2 tablespoons olive oil
2 cloves garlic, minced
2 teaspoons dried thyme
2 teaspoons dried rosemary
1 teaspoon smoked paprika
1/2 teaspoon salt
1/4 teaspoon black pepper

Instructions:

Preheat your grill to medium-high heat.
In a small bowl, whisk together the olive oil, minced garlic, dried thyme, dried rosemary, smoked paprika, salt, and black pepper.
Rub the mixture all over the pork tenderloin, making sure to coat it evenly.
Place the pork tenderloin on the grill and cook for 10-12 minutes per side, or until the internal temperature reaches 145°F.
Remove the pork tenderloin from the grill and let it rest for a few minutes before slicing and serving.
Serve with your favorite sides, such as grilled vegetables or a salad.
Enjoy your delicious grilled pork tenderloin!

Grilled Bruschetta Chicken

Ingredients:

4 boneless, skinless chicken breasts
2 tablespoons olive oil
1 teaspoon dried basil
1 teaspoon dried oregano
1/2 teaspoon garlic powder
Salt and pepper
1 large tomato, diced
2 cloves garlic, minced
1/4 cup chopped fresh basil
1 tablespoon balsamic vinegar
1 tablespoon olive oil
Salt and pepper
4 slices of Italian bread
1/4 cup shredded Parmesan cheese

Instructions:

Preheat your grill to medium-high heat.
In a small bowl, whisk together 2 tablespoons of olive oil, dried basil, dried oregano, garlic powder, salt, and pepper. Rub the mixture all over the chicken breasts.
In another small bowl, combine the diced tomato, minced garlic, chopped fresh basil, balsamic vinegar, 1 tablespoon of olive oil, salt, and pepper. Stir to combine and set aside.
Grill the chicken breasts for 6-8 minutes per side, or until the internal temperature reaches 165°F.
While the chicken is cooking, brush the slices of Italian bread with olive oil and grill for 1-2 minutes per side, or until toasted.
Top each slice of grilled bread with a chicken breast, then spoon the tomato mixture over the chicken.
Sprinkle each chicken breast with shredded Parmesan cheese.
Serve hot and enjoy your delicious grilled bruschetta chicken!
Note: You can also add a drizzle of balsamic glaze over the top for an extra burst of flavor.

Honey Balsamic Grilled Chicken Thighs

Ingredients:

4 bone-in, skin-on chicken thighs
1/4 cup balsamic vinegar
2 tablespoons honey
2 tablespoons olive oil
1 tablespoon Dijon mustard
2 cloves garlic, minced
1/2 teaspoon dried oregano
Salt and pepper
Chopped fresh parsley, for garnish

Instructions:

In a small bowl, whisk together the balsamic vinegar, honey, olive oil, Dijon mustard, minced garlic, dried oregano, salt, and pepper.
Place the chicken thighs in a large resealable plastic bag and pour the marinade over them. Seal the bag and toss to coat the chicken evenly. Refrigerate for at least 30 minutes, or up to 4 hours.
Preheat your grill to medium-high heat.
Remove the chicken from the marinade and discard any excess marinade.
Place the chicken on the grill, skin side down, and cook for 6-8 minutes per side, or until the internal temperature reaches 165°F and the skin is crispy and browned.
Brush the chicken with any remaining marinade during the last few minutes of grilling.
Remove the chicken from the grill and let it rest for a few minutes before serving.
Garnish with chopped fresh parsley before serving.
Enjoy your delicious honey balsamic grilled chicken thighs!

Sticky Grilled Chicken

Ingredients:

4 boneless, skinless chicken breasts
1/4 cup honey
1/4 cup soy sauce
2 tablespoons brown sugar
2 tablespoons olive oil
2 tablespoons rice vinegar
2 cloves garlic, minced
1 teaspoon grated ginger
Salt and pepper
Chopped scallions, for garnish
Sesame seeds, for garnish

Instructions:

In a small bowl, whisk together the honey, soy sauce, brown sugar, olive oil, rice vinegar, minced garlic, grated ginger, salt, and pepper.
Place the chicken breasts in a large resealable plastic bag and pour the marinade over them. Seal the bag and toss to coat the chicken evenly. Refrigerate for at least 30 minutes, or up to 4 hours.
Preheat your grill to medium-high heat.
Remove the chicken from the marinade and discard any excess marinade.
Place the chicken on the grill and cook for 5-6 minutes per side, or until the internal temperature reaches 165°F.
Brush the chicken with any remaining marinade during the last few minutes of grilling.
Remove the chicken from the grill and let it rest for a few minutes before slicing.
Garnish with chopped scallions and sesame seeds before serving.
Enjoy your delicious sticky grilled chicken!

Grilled Chicken Wings

Ingredients:

2 pounds chicken wings, separated at the joints, tips removed
1/4 cup olive oil
2 tablespoons soy sauce
2 cloves garlic, minced
1 teaspoon smoked paprika
1/2 teaspoon salt
1/4 teaspoon black pepper
Optional: hot sauce or BBQ sauce, for serving

Instructions:

In a large bowl, whisk together the olive oil, soy sauce, minced garlic, smoked paprika, salt, and pepper.
Add the chicken wings to the bowl and toss to coat them evenly in the marinade. Cover the bowl with plastic wrap and refrigerate for at least 30 minutes, or up to 4 hours.
Preheat your grill to medium-high heat.
Remove the chicken wings from the marinade and discard any excess marinade.
Place the chicken wings on the grill and cook for 8-10 minutes per side, or until the skin is crispy and browned and the internal temperature reaches 165°F.
Brush the chicken wings with any remaining marinade or your favorite hot sauce or BBQ sauce during the last few minutes of grilling.
Remove the chicken wings from the grill and let them rest for a few minutes before serving.
Serve with additional hot sauce or BBQ sauce, if desired.
Enjoy your delicious grilled chicken wings!

Grilled Lobster Tails

Ingredients:

4 lobster tails, 6-8 ounces each
1/2 cup melted butter
2 cloves garlic, minced
1 tablespoon lemon juice
Salt and pepper
Chopped fresh parsley, for garnish
Lemon wedges, for serving

Instructions:

Preheat your grill to medium-high heat.
Use a pair of kitchen shears to cut down the back of each lobster tail, stopping at the tail fin.
Carefully use your hands to gently pull apart the shell, exposing the meat.
In a small bowl, whisk together the melted butter, minced garlic, and lemon juice.
Brush the butter mixture generously over the lobster meat, making sure to get into all the nooks and crannies.
Season the lobster tails with salt and pepper to taste.
Carefully place the lobster tails on the grill, meat side down. Grill for 5-7 minutes, or until the meat is opaque and lightly charred.
Use tongs to carefully flip the lobster tails over and grill for an additional 2-3 minutes on the shell side.
Remove the lobster tails from the grill and transfer to a platter.
Garnish with chopped parsley and serve with lemon wedges on the side.
Enjoy your delicious grilled lobster tails!

Grilled Broccoli

Ingredients:

1 pound fresh broccoli, trimmed into florets
2 tablespoons olive oil
1 teaspoon salt
1/2 teaspoon black pepper
2 garlic cloves, minced
1 tablespoon lemon juice
1/4 cup grated Parmesan cheese (optional)

Instructions:

Preheat the grill to medium-high heat.
In a large bowl, toss the broccoli florets with the olive oil, salt, black pepper, and minced garlic until they are well coated.
Place the broccoli florets on the grill and cook for 5-7 minutes, turning occasionally, until they are tender and slightly charred.
Remove the broccoli from the grill and transfer to a serving platter.
Drizzle the lemon juice over the broccoli and sprinkle with grated Parmesan cheese, if using.
Serve the grilled broccoli as a side dish. It pairs well with grilled meats or fish.
Enjoy your delicious Grilled Broccoli!

Grilled Pizza

Ingredients:

1 pound pizza dough
1/2 cup pizza sauce
2 cups shredded mozzarella cheese
Toppings of your choice (e.g. pepperoni, sliced vegetables, cooked sausage, etc.)
Olive oil
Salt and pepper
Flour, for dusting

Instructions:

Preheat your grill to medium-high heat.
Dust a clean surface with flour and roll out the pizza dough into a circle or rectangle, about 1/4 inch thick.
Brush one side of the dough with olive oil and sprinkle with salt and pepper.
Carefully place the oiled side of the dough onto the grill grates and cook for 2-3 minutes, or until the bottom is lightly charred and the dough has puffed up slightly.
Use a pair of tongs to carefully flip the dough over and grill for an additional 1-2 minutes on the other side.
Remove the grilled pizza crust from the grill and place it on a cutting board or pizza pan.
Spread pizza sauce over the grilled crust, leaving a small border around the edges.
Sprinkle shredded mozzarella cheese over the sauce, followed by your desired toppings.
Return the pizza to the grill and cook for an additional 5-7 minutes, or until the cheese is melted and bubbly and the toppings are cooked to your liking.
Use a pizza cutter or sharp knife to slice the grilled pizza into pieces and serve immediately.
Enjoy your delicious grilled pizza!

Grilled Baked Potatoes

Ingredients:

4 large potatoes (russet or Idaho)
2 tablespoons olive oil
1 teaspoon salt
1/2 teaspoon black pepper
1/4 cup grated Parmesan cheese
2 tablespoons chopped fresh parsley
2 tablespoons chopped fresh chives
2 garlic cloves, minced

Instructions:

Preheat the grill to medium-high heat.
Wash the potatoes thoroughly and pat them dry with a paper towel.
Cut each potato into thick slices (about 1/2 inch thick).
In a large bowl, mix together the olive oil, salt, black pepper, Parmesan cheese, parsley, chives, and minced garlic.
Add the potato slices to the bowl and toss until they are well coated with the oil mixture.
Place the potato slices on the grill and cook for 5-7 minutes per side, or until they are golden brown and tender when pierced with a fork.
Remove the potatoes from the grill and let them cool for a few minutes before serving.
Serve the grilled baked potatoes as a side dish or appetizer. They pair well with grilled meats or vegetables.
Enjoy your delicious Grilled Baked Potatoes!

Chicken Souvlaki

Ingredients:

1 1/2 pounds boneless, skinless chicken breasts, cut into bite-sized pieces
1/4 cup olive oil
1/4 cup lemon juice
1 tablespoon red wine vinegar
1 teaspoon dried oregano
1 teaspoon dried thyme
1 teaspoon paprika
1/2 teaspoon garlic powder
Salt and black pepper, to taste
Wooden skewers, soaked in water for at least 30 minutes before grilling
Tzatziki sauce, for serving (optional)

Instructions:

In a medium bowl, whisk together olive oil, lemon juice, red wine vinegar, dried oregano, dried thyme, paprika, garlic powder, salt, and black pepper.
Add the chicken pieces to the bowl and toss to coat evenly. Cover the bowl with plastic wrap and refrigerate for at least 30 minutes, or up to 4 hours to marinate.
Preheat your grill to medium-high heat.
Once the grill is hot, thread the chicken pieces onto the wooden skewers, leaving a little space in between each piece.
Place the chicken skewers on the grill and cook for about 5-7 minutes per side, or until the chicken is cooked through and slightly charred on the outside.
Once the chicken is done, remove the skewers from the grill and transfer to a serving dish.
Serve the Chicken Souvlaki with tzatziki sauce on the side for dipping, and enjoy!
Note: You can also serve the Chicken Souvlaki with pita bread, sliced tomatoes, cucumbers, and red onions for a complete meal. And if you don't have wooden skewers, you can also use metal skewers.

Grilled Green Beans

Ingredients:

1 pound fresh green beans, trimmed
2 tablespoons olive oil
1 teaspoon salt
1/2 teaspoon black pepper
1/4 cup grated Parmesan cheese
1 teaspoon garlic powder
1 teaspoon onion powder
1/4 teaspoon red pepper flakes (optional)

Instructions:

Preheat the grill to medium-high heat.
In a large bowl, toss the green beans with the olive oil, salt, and black pepper until they are well coated.
Place the green beans on the grill and cook for 5-7 minutes, turning occasionally, until they are tender and slightly charred.
In a small bowl, mix together the grated Parmesan cheese, garlic powder, onion powder, and red pepper flakes (if using).
When the green beans are cooked, transfer them to a serving platter and sprinkle the Parmesan cheese mixture over the top.
Toss the green beans with the Parmesan cheese mixture until they are well coated.
Serve the grilled green beans as a side dish or appetizer. They pair well with grilled meats or fish.
Enjoy your delicious Grilled Green Beans!

Grilled Shrimp Foil Packets

Ingredients:

1 pound large raw shrimp, peeled and deveined
2 tablespoons olive oil
2 cloves garlic, minced
1 teaspoon paprika
1/2 teaspoon onion powder
1/4 teaspoon cayenne pepper
Salt and black pepper, to taste
1 red bell pepper, seeded and sliced
1 yellow onion, sliced
1 zucchini, sliced
1 lemon, sliced
Fresh parsley, chopped, for serving

Instructions:

Preheat your grill to medium-high heat.
In a small bowl, whisk together olive oil, minced garlic, paprika, onion powder, cayenne pepper, salt, and black pepper.
Cut 4 sheets of aluminum foil, each about 12 inches long. Divide the sliced bell pepper, onion, and zucchini evenly among the foil sheets, placing them in the center of each sheet.
Top the vegetables with the raw shrimp. Drizzle the olive oil and spice mixture over the shrimp and vegetables, then add a couple of lemon slices to each packet.
Fold up the sides of the foil packets, leaving some space for steam to circulate. Seal the packets tightly.
Place the foil packets on the grill and cook for about 10-12 minutes, or until the shrimp are pink and opaque and the vegetables are tender.
Carefully open the foil packets and transfer the shrimp and vegetables to a serving dish. Sprinkle with fresh chopped parsley and serve immediately.
Note: You can also use other vegetables such as cherry tomatoes, asparagus, or mushrooms depending on your preference. And feel free to adjust the seasonings to taste.

Cilantro Lime Grilled Salmon

Ingredients:

4 salmon fillets, skin-on
1/4 cup olive oil
1/4 cup chopped fresh cilantro
2 cloves garlic, minced
2 tablespoons lime juice
1 teaspoon honey
1/2 teaspoon salt
1/4 teaspoon black pepper
Lime wedges, for serving

Instructions:

In a small bowl, whisk together olive oil, chopped cilantro, minced garlic, lime juice, honey, salt, and black pepper.
Place the salmon fillets in a shallow dish and pour the marinade over the top, making sure to coat the salmon evenly. Cover the dish with plastic wrap and refrigerate for at least 30 minutes, or up to 2 hours.
Preheat your grill to medium-high heat.
Once the grill is hot, remove the salmon fillets from the marinade and shake off any excess.
Place the salmon fillets on the grill, skin-side down, and cook for about 5-6 minutes.
Carefully flip the salmon fillets over and continue to cook for another 3-4 minutes, or until the salmon is cooked through and slightly charred on the outside.
Once the salmon is done, remove from the grill and transfer to a serving dish.
Serve the Cilantro Lime Grilled Salmon with lime wedges on the side for squeezing over the top, and enjoy!
Note: You can also serve the Cilantro Lime Grilled Salmon with a side of rice, roasted vegetables, or a simple green salad for a complete meal. And if you prefer, you can also grill the salmon on a piece of foil or a cedar plank for added flavor.

Mediterranean Grilled Eggplant

Ingredients:

1 large eggplant, sliced into 1/2-inch rounds
1/4 cup olive oil
1 tablespoon red wine vinegar
2 cloves garlic, minced
1 teaspoon dried oregano
Salt and black pepper, to taste
Lemon wedges, for serving
Crumbled feta cheese, for serving (optional)

Instructions:

Preheat your grill to medium-high heat.
In a small bowl, whisk together olive oil, red wine vinegar, minced garlic, dried oregano, salt, and black pepper.
Brush the eggplant slices with the olive oil mixture, making sure to coat both sides evenly.
Place the eggplant slices on the grill and cook for about 3-4 minutes per side, or until the eggplant is tender and slightly charred on the outside.
Once the eggplant is done, remove from the grill and transfer to a serving dish.
Serve the Mediterranean Grilled Eggplant with lemon wedges on the side for squeezing over the top, and crumbled feta cheese (if using) for an extra burst of flavor.
Note: You can also add sliced tomatoes, chopped fresh herbs (such as parsley or basil), and olives to the dish for a more complete Mediterranean-inspired appetizer or side dish.

Best Grilled Chicken Breast

Ingredients:

4 boneless, skinless chicken breasts
1/4 cup olive oil
2 tablespoons lemon juice
2 cloves garlic, minced
1 teaspoon dried thyme
1 teaspoon dried rosemary
1/2 teaspoon salt
1/4 teaspoon black pepper

Instructions:

Preheat your grill to medium-high heat.
In a small bowl, whisk together olive oil, lemon juice, minced garlic, dried thyme, dried rosemary, salt, and black pepper.
Place the chicken breasts in a shallow dish or large resealable bag. Pour the marinade over the chicken and toss to coat. Let the chicken marinate for at least 30 minutes, or up to 4 hours in the refrigerator.
Once the grill is hot, remove the chicken from the marinade and discard any remaining marinade.
Place the chicken breasts on the grill and cook for about 5-6 minutes per side, or until the internal temperature of the chicken reaches 165°F (75°C) on an instant-read thermometer.
Once the chicken is cooked through, remove it from the grill and let it rest for a few minutes before serving.
Serve the grilled chicken breasts with your favorite sides and enjoy!
Note: For best results, make sure to let the chicken come to room temperature for 15-20 minutes before grilling, and make sure to oil the grill grates before cooking to prevent sticking.

Grilled Scallops

Ingredients:

1 pound fresh scallops, rinsed and patted dry
2 tablespoons olive oil
1 teaspoon salt
1/2 teaspoon black pepper
2 garlic cloves, minced
2 tablespoons chopped fresh parsley
2 tablespoons lemon juice

Instructions:

Preheat the grill to medium-high heat.
In a large bowl, mix together the olive oil, salt, black pepper, minced garlic, chopped parsley, and lemon juice.
Add the scallops to the bowl and toss until they are well coated with the oil mixture.
Thread the scallops onto skewers, making sure to leave a small gap between each one.
Place the skewers on the grill and cook for 2-3 minutes per side, or until the scallops are opaque and slightly firm to the touch.
Remove the scallops from the grill and let them rest for a few minutes before serving.
Serve the grilled scallops as a main dish or appetizer. They pair well with a simple green salad or grilled vegetables.
Enjoy your delicious Grilled Scallops!

Grilled Potatoes

Ingredients:

1 1/2 pounds baby potatoes (or small Yukon gold or red potatoes), halved
2 tablespoons olive oil
1 tablespoon chopped fresh rosemary
1 tablespoon chopped fresh thyme
1/2 teaspoon garlic powder
Salt and black pepper, to taste

Instructions:

Preheat your grill to medium-high heat.
In a large bowl, combine halved potatoes, olive oil, chopped rosemary, chopped thyme, garlic powder, salt, and black pepper. Toss to coat evenly.
Cut a sheet of aluminum foil, about 18 inches long. Place the seasoned potatoes on the center of the foil sheet.
Fold the foil over the potatoes and seal the edges tightly to create a packet.
Place the foil packet on the grill and cook for about 20-25 minutes, or until the potatoes are tender when pierced with a fork. Flip the packet halfway through cooking to ensure even cooking.
Once the potatoes are done, carefully open the foil packet and transfer the potatoes to a serving dish. Serve immediately and enjoy!
Note: You can also add sliced onions, bell peppers or mushrooms to the packet to add some extra flavor and texture. And if you prefer crispy potatoes, you can grill them without the foil directly on the grates, but make sure to keep an eye on them as they can burn easily.

Sweet Chili-Lime Grilled Chicken

Ingredients:

4 boneless, skinless chicken breasts
1/4 cup sweet chili sauce
2 tablespoons lime juice
1 tablespoon soy sauce
1 tablespoon honey
1 teaspoon garlic powder
1/2 teaspoon salt
1/4 teaspoon black pepper
Lime wedges, for serving

Instructions:

In a small bowl, whisk together sweet chili sauce, lime juice, soy sauce, honey, garlic powder, salt, and black pepper.
Place the chicken breasts in a shallow dish or large resealable bag. Pour the marinade over the chicken and toss to coat. Let the chicken marinate for at least 30 minutes, or up to 4 hours in the refrigerator.
Preheat your grill to medium-high heat.
Once the grill is hot, remove the chicken from the marinade and discard any remaining marinade.
Place the chicken breasts on the grill and cook for about 5-6 minutes per side, or until the internal temperature of the chicken reaches 165°F (75°C) on an instant-read thermometer.
Once the chicken is cooked through, remove it from the grill and let it rest for a few minutes before serving.
Serve the Sweet Chili-Lime Grilled Chicken with lime wedges on the side for squeezing over the top, and enjoy!
Note: For best results, make sure to let the chicken come to room temperature for 15-20 minutes before grilling, and make sure to oil the grill grates before cooking to prevent sticking. You can also garnish the chicken with sliced green onions or chopped cilantro, if desired.

Chipotle Tofu & Pineapple Skewers

Ingredients:

1 block of firm tofu, drained and cut into 1-inch cubes
1/2 a fresh pineapple, cut into 1-inch cubes
1 red onion, cut into 1-inch cubes
2 tablespoons of olive oil
1 tablespoon of adobo sauce (from canned chipotle peppers)
1 teaspoon of honey
1 teaspoon of smoked paprika
1/2 teaspoon of garlic powder
Salt and black pepper, to taste
8-10 skewers (if using wooden skewers, soak them in water for at least 30 minutes before grilling)

Instructions:
In a small bowl, whisk together olive oil, adobo sauce, honey, smoked paprika, garlic powder, salt, and black pepper.
Thread the tofu, pineapple, and onion onto the skewers, alternating between them.
Brush the skewers with the chipotle marinade, making sure to coat them evenly.
Preheat your grill to medium-high heat. Once the grill is hot, place the skewers on the grill and cook for about 10-12 minutes, turning occasionally, until the tofu and pineapple are lightly charred and cooked through.
Once the skewers are cooked, remove them from the grill and place them on a serving dish.
Serve the skewers hot and enjoy!
Note: If you don't have access to fresh pineapple, you can use canned pineapple chunks instead. Just make sure to drain them well before using.

Summer Panzanella

Ingredients:

1 small baguette, cut into bite-sized cubes
3 tablespoons olive oil, divided
Salt and black pepper, to taste
1 pint cherry tomatoes, halved
1 large cucumber, diced
1/2 red onion, thinly sliced
1/2 cup fresh basil leaves, torn into pieces
1/2 cup fresh mozzarella balls, halved
2 tablespoons red wine vinegar
1 garlic clove, minced

Instructions:

Preheat your oven to 375°F (190°C).
Toss the cubed bread with 2 tablespoons of olive oil, salt, and black pepper. Spread the bread cubes in a single layer on a baking sheet and bake for about 10-12 minutes, or until the bread is lightly toasted and crispy.
While the bread is toasting, prepare the other ingredients. In a large bowl, combine cherry tomatoes, cucumber, red onion, torn basil leaves, and fresh mozzarella.
In a small bowl, whisk together red wine vinegar, minced garlic, remaining 1 tablespoon of olive oil, salt, and black pepper.
Once the bread cubes are toasted, add them to the bowl with the other ingredients. Pour the dressing over the top and toss everything together until well combined.
Let the salad sit for about 15-20 minutes before serving, to allow the flavors to meld together.
Serve the Summer Panzanella salad as a main dish or as a side dish with your favorite grilled protein, and enjoy!
Note: You can customize this recipe by adding or substituting other vegetables or herbs, such as bell peppers, olives, or parsley, depending on your taste preferences.

Grilled Beer Brats

Ingredients:

6 bratwurst sausages
1 large onion, thinly sliced
2 cloves garlic, minced
1 tablespoon olive oil
1 cup beer (pilsner or lager)
1 tablespoon whole grain mustard
1 teaspoon smoked paprika
Salt and pepper, to taste
6 hot dog buns
Optional toppings: sauerkraut, chopped fresh parsley, additional mustard

Instructions:

Preheat a grill to medium-high heat.
In a large skillet, heat the olive oil over medium heat. Add the sliced onion and garlic and cook, stirring occasionally, for 5-7 minutes or until the onion is soft and translucent.
Pour in the beer, mustard, and smoked paprika, and stir to combine. Let the mixture simmer for a few minutes until the liquid has reduced slightly.

Add the bratwurst sausages to the skillet, and turn to coat them with the beer mixture. Let them cook for 5-7 minutes, turning occasionally, until browned on all sides.
Remove the brats from the skillet and transfer them to the grill. Cook them on the grill, turning occasionally, for another 5-7 minutes or until they are cooked through and have nice grill marks.
While the brats are grilling, toast the hot dog buns on the grill for a few seconds.
To assemble the brats, place each sausage in a bun and top with the beer-braised onions. Add any additional toppings of your choice, such as sauerkraut, chopped fresh parsley, or more mustard.
Serve hot and enjoy your delicious grilled beer brats!

Grilled Corn

Ingredients:

4 ears of corn, husks removed
2 tablespoons of olive oil
1 teaspoon of salt
1/2 teaspoon of black pepper
1/2 teaspoon of chili powder
1/4 cup of freshly chopped cilantro
1 lime, cut into wedges

Instructions:

Preheat your grill to medium-high heat.
Brush each ear of corn with olive oil, making sure to cover all sides.
In a small bowl, mix together salt, black pepper, and chili powder. Sprinkle the mixture over the ears of corn, ensuring that they are well-coated.
Place the ears of corn on the grill and cook for about 10-12 minutes, turning occasionally, until the corn is cooked through and slightly charred.
Once the corn is cooked, remove it from the grill and place it on a serving dish.
Sprinkle chopped cilantro over the corn and squeeze a lime wedge over each ear.
Serve the grilled corn hot and enjoy!

Mahi Mahi Tacos

Ingredients:

1 lb. Mahi Mahi fillets, cut into small pieces
2 tablespoons olive oil
1 tablespoon chili powder
1/2 teaspoon garlic powder
1/2 teaspoon cumin
1/2 teaspoon smoked paprika
Salt and pepper
8 corn tortillas
1 avocado, sliced
1/2 red onion, sliced

For the slaw:

2 cups thinly sliced cabbage
1/2 cup thinly sliced red onion
1/4 cup chopped fresh cilantro
2 tablespoons lime juice
1 tablespoon olive oil
Salt and pepper

Instructions:

Preheat a skillet over medium-high heat.
In a small bowl, mix together the olive oil, chili powder, garlic powder, cumin, smoked paprika, salt, and pepper.
Add the Mahi Mahi pieces to the skillet and pour the spice mixture over them. Cook for 5-7 minutes or until the fish is cooked through, stirring occasionally.
While the fish is cooking, make the slaw by combining the cabbage, red onion, cilantro, lime juice, olive oil, salt, and pepper in a bowl. Mix well and set aside.
Heat the corn tortillas in a separate skillet or on the grill until they are warm and slightly charred.
To assemble the tacos, place some of the Mahi Mahi on each tortilla followed by some of the slaw, avocado slices, red onion slices, and chopped cilantro.
Squeeze some lime juice over the top of each taco and serve immediately.
Enjoy your delicious Mahi Mahi tacos!

Honey Soy Grilled Pork Chops

Ingredients:

4 pork chops
1/4 cup honey
1/4 cup soy sauce
2 tablespoons vegetable oil
2 cloves garlic, minced
1/2 teaspoon ground ginger
Salt and pepper

Instructions:

Preheat your grill to medium-high heat.
In a small bowl, whisk together the honey, soy sauce, vegetable oil, garlic, and ground ginger to make the marinade.
Season the pork chops with salt and pepper on both sides.
Place the pork chops in a shallow dish or large resealable bag and pour the marinade over them.
Make sure the pork chops are fully coated in the marinade.
Cover the dish or seal the bag and refrigerate for at least 30 minutes or up to 4 hours to allow the pork chops to marinate.
Remove the pork chops from the marinade and discard any excess marinade.
Place the pork chops on the grill and cook for 5-6 minutes on each side or until they reach an internal temperature of 145°F.
Let the pork chops rest for a few minutes before serving to allow the juices to redistribute.
Serve the pork chops with your favorite side dishes and enjoy!
Note: You can also baste the pork chops with the leftover marinade while grilling for added flavor.

BBQ Tempeh Sandwiches

Ingredients:

1 package of tempeh, sliced into thin strips
1/2 cup of your favorite BBQ sauce
2 tablespoons apple cider vinegar
1 tablespoon olive oil
1/2 teaspoon garlic powder
1/2 teaspoon onion powder
Salt and pepper
4 hamburger buns
Sliced red onion (optional)
Sliced pickles (optional)
Coleslaw (optional)

Instructions:

Preheat a skillet over medium-high heat.
In a small bowl, whisk together the BBQ sauce, apple cider vinegar, olive oil, garlic powder, onion powder, salt, and pepper.
Add the sliced tempeh to the skillet and pour the BBQ sauce mixture over the top. Stir to coat the tempeh.
Cook the tempeh for 5-7 minutes or until it is crispy and golden brown, stirring occasionally.
While the tempeh is cooking, toast the hamburger buns on a separate skillet or on the grill.
To assemble the sandwiches, place some of the BBQ tempeh on the bottom half of each bun. Add some sliced red onion, pickles, and coleslaw if desired.
Top with the other half of the bun and serve immediately.
Enjoy your delicious BBQ tempeh sandwiches!

Grilled Chicken Kebab

Ingredients:

1 pound boneless, skinless chicken breasts, cut into 1-inch cubes
1/4 cup olive oil
2 tablespoons fresh lemon juice
2 cloves garlic, minced
1 teaspoon paprika
1 teaspoon ground cumin
1/2 teaspoon salt
1/4 teaspoon black pepper
Wooden or metal skewers
Optional: diced onion, bell pepper, and/or cherry tomatoes for skewering

Instructions:

If using wooden skewers, soak them in water for at least 30 minutes to prevent burning during grilling.
In a small bowl, whisk together the olive oil, lemon juice, garlic, paprika, cumin, salt, and black pepper.
Place the chicken cubes in a large zip-top bag and pour the marinade over the top. Seal the bag and refrigerate for at least 1 hour (or up to 8 hours) to allow the flavors to penetrate the meat.
Preheat a grill to medium-high heat.
If using vegetables, thread them onto skewers along with the marinated chicken cubes.
Grill the chicken kebabs for 10-12 minutes, turning occasionally, until the chicken is cooked through and slightly charred on the outside.
Serve hot, garnished with fresh herbs and a squeeze of lemon juice, if desired. Enjoy!

Grilled Brie with Wine

Ingredients:

1 wheel of Brie cheese
1 tablespoon olive oil
1/4 cup dry white wine
2 tablespoons honey
Fresh herbs (such as thyme or rosemary), for garnish
Baguette slices or crackers, for serving

Instructions:

Preheat your grill to medium-high heat.
While the grill is heating, remove any packaging or wrapping from the Brie cheese. Leave the rind intact, as it will help hold the cheese together while grilling.
Brush the Brie cheese with olive oil on both sides. This will help prevent sticking and add flavor.
Place the Brie cheese directly on the grill grates. Close the lid and grill for about 3-4 minutes per side, or until the cheese starts to soften and melt slightly.
While the Brie is grilling, in a small saucepan over low heat, combine the white wine and honey. Stir until the honey is dissolved and the mixture is warmed through.
Remove the Brie from the grill and transfer it to a serving platter or plate.
Drizzle the warm honey-wine mixture over the grilled Brie. The mixture will seep into the cheese, adding a sweet and tangy flavor.
Garnish the Brie with fresh herbs, such as thyme or rosemary, for added fragrance and visual appeal.
Serve the grilled Brie with baguette slices or crackers on the side, allowing your guests to spread the warm, melted cheese onto the bread.
Enjoy your delicious Grilled Brie with Wine!

Classic Burger

Ingredients:

1 lb. ground beef (80/20 or 85/15)
4 hamburger buns
4 slices of cheese (optional)
4 lettuce leaves
4 tomato slices
1/2 onion, sliced
Ketchup and mustard (optional)
Salt and pepper

Instructions:

Preheat your grill or skillet to medium-high heat.
Divide the ground beef into four equal portions and shape them into patties that are about 1/2 inch thick.
Season the patties with salt and pepper on both sides.
Place the patties on the grill or skillet and cook for about 4-5 minutes on each side or until they are cooked to your desired level of doneness.
If you want to add cheese to your burgers, place a slice on each patty during the last minute of cooking to allow it to melt.
While the patties are cooking, toast the hamburger buns on the grill or skillet until they are lightly browned.
To assemble the burgers, place a lettuce leaf on the bottom half of each bun followed by a tomato slice and some onion slices.
Add the cooked patty on top and then add ketchup and mustard if desired.
Top with the other half of the bun and serve immediately.
Enjoy your delicious classic burger!

Ribs On The Grill

Ingredients:

2 racks of baby back ribs
1 cup of your favorite BBQ sauce
1/4 cup brown sugar
2 tablespoons paprika
2 tablespoons garlic powder
1 tablespoon onion powder
1 tablespoon salt
1 teaspoon black pepper

Instructions:

Preheat your grill to medium heat (around 300-350°F).
While the grill is heating up, prepare the ribs. Remove the membrane from the back of the ribs by running a butter knife under it and pulling it off.
In a small bowl, mix together the brown sugar, paprika, garlic powder, onion powder, salt, and black pepper.
Rub the spice mixture all over the ribs, making sure to coat them evenly.
Place the ribs on the grill, bone side down, and cover with the lid.
Cook the ribs for about 1.5 to 2 hours, turning them every 30 minutes or so.
After about 1.5 hours, start basting the ribs with the BBQ sauce every 10-15 minutes.
Continue cooking until the ribs are tender and the meat is starting to pull away from the bone.
Remove the ribs from the grill and let them rest for 5-10 minutes before slicing and serving.
Enjoy your delicious grilled ribs!

Summer Panzanella

Ingredients:

4 cups day-old crusty bread, cut into cubes
2 tablespoons extra-virgin olive oil
2 cloves garlic, minced
2 cups ripe tomatoes, diced
1 cucumber, seeded and diced
1 red bell pepper, diced
1/2 red onion, thinly sliced
1/4 cup fresh basil leaves, torn
1/4 cup fresh parsley leaves, chopped
1/4 cup Kalamata olives, pitted and halved
3 tablespoons red wine vinegar
Salt and pepper, to taste

Instructions:

Preheat your oven to 375°F (190°C).

In a large bowl, toss the bread cubes with olive oil and minced garlic. Spread the bread cubes on a baking sheet and toast in the preheated oven for about 10-15 minutes, or until they are golden brown and crispy. Set aside to cool.
In a large mixing bowl, combine the diced tomatoes, cucumber, red bell pepper, red onion, torn basil leaves, chopped parsley, and halved Kalamata olives.
Add the cooled toasted bread cubes to the bowl with the vegetable mixture.
Drizzle the red wine vinegar over the salad. Season with salt and pepper to taste. Toss everything together gently until well combined, making sure the bread is coated with the dressing.
Let the Summer Panzanella sit for about 15 minutes to allow the flavors to meld together and the bread to soak up the dressing.
Serve the Summer Panzanella as a refreshing salad or as a side dish for grilled meats or seafood. It's best enjoyed at room temperature.
The Summer Panzanella is a vibrant and flavorful salad that showcases the fresh produce of the season. The combination of crispy bread, juicy tomatoes, crunchy cucumbers, and tangy dressing creates a delicious and satisfying dish. Enjoy!

Spicy Coconut Grilled Chicken

Ingredients:

4 boneless, skinless chicken breasts
1 cup coconut milk
2 tablespoons soy sauce
2 tablespoons lime juice
2 tablespoons Sriracha sauce (adjust to taste)
2 cloves garlic, minced
1 tablespoon brown sugar
1 teaspoon ground cumin
1 teaspoon ground coriander
1/2 teaspoon turmeric
Salt and pepper, to taste
Fresh cilantro, chopped (for garnish)
Lime wedges (for serving)

Instructions:

In a mixing bowl, combine the coconut milk, soy sauce, lime juice, Sriracha sauce, minced garlic, brown sugar, cumin, coriander, turmeric, salt, and pepper. Whisk well to combine and create the marinade.
Place the chicken breasts in a shallow dish or a resealable plastic bag. Pour the marinade over the chicken, making sure each piece is coated evenly. If using a dish, cover with plastic wrap. If using a bag, seal it and gently massage the marinade into the chicken. Marinate in the refrigerator for at least 2 hours, or overnight for best results.
Preheat your grill to medium-high heat.
Remove the chicken from the marinade and let any excess marinade drip off. Discard the remaining marinade.
Grill the chicken breasts for about 6-8 minutes per side, or until they are cooked through and have reached an internal temperature of 165°F (75°C). The cooking time may vary depending on the thickness of the chicken breasts. Baste the chicken with any remaining marinade during grilling for extra flavor.
Once cooked, remove the chicken from the grill and let it rest for a few minutes.
Garnish the Spicy Coconut Grilled Chicken with freshly chopped cilantro. Serve with lime wedges on the side for squeezing over the chicken for added freshness.
You can enjoy the Spicy Coconut Grilled Chicken with a side of rice, salad, or grilled vegetables. It's a flavorful and delicious dish with a hint of heat from the Sriracha and a touch of creaminess from the coconut milk. Enjoy!

Gnocchi Foil Packets

Ingredients:

1 pound store-bought gnocchi
1 cup cherry tomatoes, halved
1 zucchini, sliced
1 yellow squash, sliced
1 bell pepper, sliced
1 small red onion, sliced
4 cloves garlic, minced
4 tablespoons olive oil
1 teaspoon Italian seasoning
Salt and pepper, to taste
Fresh basil leaves, torn (for garnish)
Grated Parmesan cheese (optional)

Instructions:

Preheat your grill to medium heat.
Tear off four large sheets of aluminum foil, each about 12 inches long.
In a large bowl, combine the gnocchi, cherry tomatoes, zucchini, yellow squash, bell pepper, red onion, minced garlic, olive oil, Italian seasoning, salt, and pepper. Toss everything together until well coated.
Divide the gnocchi and vegetable mixture evenly among the four sheets of foil, placing the mixture in the center of each sheet.
Fold the sides of each foil sheet over the gnocchi and vegetables, sealing them tightly to form packets.
Place the foil packets on the preheated grill and cook for about 12-15 minutes, or until the gnocchi is cooked through and the vegetables are tender. Be careful when opening the foil packets as the steam inside will be hot.
Carefully open the foil packets and transfer the contents to serving plates.
Garnish the Gnocchi Foil Packets with torn basil leaves and grated Parmesan cheese, if desired.
Serve the Gnocchi Foil Packets as a complete meal or as a side dish. They are delicious on their own, but you can also pair them with a fresh salad or crusty bread.
Gnocchi Foil Packets are a convenient and flavorful way to cook gnocchi and vegetables together. The foil helps to trap the heat and steam, allowing the ingredients to cook and infuse with each other's flavors. Enjoy!

Grilled Oysters

Ingredients:

12 fresh oysters, in the shell
4 tablespoons unsalted butter, melted
2 cloves garlic, minced
2 tablespoons fresh parsley, chopped
1 tablespoon fresh lemon juice
Salt and pepper, to taste
Lemon wedges, for serving

Instructions:

Preheat your grill to medium-high heat.
Scrub the oysters thoroughly under cold running water to remove any dirt or debris.
Using an oyster shucking knife, carefully pry open each oyster shell, being cautious not to spill the oyster liquor. Discard the top shell and loosen the oyster from the bottom shell, keeping it intact.
In a small bowl, combine the melted butter, minced garlic, chopped parsley, fresh lemon juice, salt, and pepper. Mix well to make the garlic butter sauce.
Place the shucked oysters on the grill grates, flat side down. Spoon about a teaspoon of the garlic butter sauce over each oyster.
Close the grill lid and cook the oysters for about 5-7 minutes, or until the edges start to curl and the oysters are cooked through. The cooking time may vary depending on the size of the oysters.
Carefully remove the grilled oysters from the grill using tongs or a spatula. Transfer them to a serving platter or individual plates.
Serve the Grilled Oysters immediately, garnished with additional chopped parsley and lemon wedges on the side for squeezing over the oysters.
Grilled Oysters are a flavorful and elegant appetizer or main course. The heat of the grill adds a smoky flavor to the briny oysters, while the garlic butter sauce enhances their natural taste. Enjoy them as is or with your favorite seafood accompaniments.

Authentic Jerk Chicken

Ingredients:

2 pounds chicken pieces (such as drumsticks, thighs, or breast)
6 green onions, chopped
4 cloves garlic, minced
2 Scotch bonnet peppers (or habanero peppers), seeded and minced
1 tablespoon fresh thyme leaves
2 tablespoons soy sauce
2 tablespoons vegetable oil
2 tablespoons brown sugar
2 tablespoons lime juice
1 tablespoon ground allspice
1 tablespoon ground black pepper
1 tablespoon ground cinnamon
1 tablespoon ground nutmeg
1 tablespoon ground ginger
1 teaspoon salt

Instructions:

In a food processor or blender, combine the green onions, garlic, Scotch bonnet peppers, thyme leaves, soy sauce, vegetable oil, brown sugar, lime juice, allspice, black pepper, cinnamon, nutmeg, ginger, and salt. Blend until you have a smooth paste.

Place the chicken pieces in a large bowl or resealable plastic bag. Pour the jerk marinade over the chicken, making sure each piece is well coated. If using a bowl, cover it with plastic wrap. If using a bag, seal it and gently massage the marinade into the chicken. Marinate in the refrigerator for at least 4 hours, or preferably overnight to allow the flavors to penetrate the meat.

Preheat your grill to medium-high heat.

Remove the chicken from the marinade and let any excess marinade drip off. Reserve the marinade for basting.

Grill the chicken pieces for about 6-8 minutes per side, or until they are cooked through and have reached an internal temperature of 165°F (75°C). While grilling, baste the chicken occasionally with the reserved marinade for extra flavor and moisture.

Once cooked, remove the chicken from the grill and let it rest for a few minutes.

Serve the Authentic Jerk Chicken hot, garnished with additional chopped green onions, if desired.

Authentic Jerk Chicken is known for its bold and spicy flavors. The combination of Scotch bonnet peppers, thyme, allspice, and other aromatic spices creates a tantalizing taste experience. Serve it with traditional Jamaican sides like rice and peas, fried plantains, or coleslaw for a complete meal. Enjoy the delicious heat of this classic dish!

Spiral Hot Dogs

Ingredients:

Hot dog sausages
Hot dog buns
Skewers or wooden sticks

Instructions:

Preheat your grill to medium-high heat.
Insert a skewer or wooden stick lengthwise into each hot dog sausage, starting at one end and pushing it through the center.
Using a sharp knife, make a diagonal cut at one end of the hot dog, about 1 inch deep
Holding the skewer or stick, rotate the hot dog while gently guiding the knife along the length of the sausage in a spiral motion. Continue cutting until you reach the other end, creating a spiral-shaped cut.
Carefully remove the skewer or stick from the hot dog, leaving the spiral shape intact.
Place the spiral-cut hot dogs on the preheated grill. Cook for about 5-7 minutes, turning them occasionally, until they are heated through and lightly charred.
While the hot dogs are grilling, you can also toast the hot dog buns on the grill for a few minutes, if desired.
Once the spiral hot dogs are cooked, remove them from the grill and let them cool slightly.
Serve the Spiral Hot Dogs in the toasted buns. You can add your favorite condiments and toppings, such as ketchup, mustard, relish, onions, or cheese.
Spiral Hot Dogs not only look fun and unique, but the spiral cuts also allow for more surface area to get caramelized and crispy on the grill. They're a playful twist on traditional hot dogs that can be enjoyed at barbecues, picnics, or any casual gathering.

Mediterranean Salmon Skewers

Ingredients:

1 pound salmon fillets, cut into 1-inch cubes
1/4 cup olive oil
2 tablespoons lemon juice
2 cloves garlic, minced
1 teaspoon dried oregano
1 teaspoon dried basil
1 teaspoon dried thyme
1/2 teaspoon salt
1/4 teaspoon black pepper
Cherry tomatoes
Red onion, cut into chunks
Yellow bell pepper, cut into chunks
Lemon wedges, for serving
Fresh parsley or dill, chopped (optional, for garnish)

Instructions:

In a bowl, whisk together the olive oil, lemon juice, minced garlic, dried oregano, dried basil, dried thyme, salt, and black pepper to make the marinade.
Place the salmon cubes in a shallow dish and pour the marinade over them. Toss gently to coat the salmon evenly. Cover the dish and let the salmon marinate in the refrigerator for at least 30 minutes, or up to 2 hours for more flavor.
Preheat your grill to medium-high heat.
Thread the marinated salmon cubes onto skewers, alternating with cherry tomatoes, chunks of red onion, and chunks of yellow bell pepper.
Grill the salmon skewers on the preheated grill, turning occasionally, for about 8-10 minutes or until the salmon is cooked through and slightly charred.
Remove the salmon skewers from the grill and let them rest for a few minutes.
Serve the Mediterranean Salmon Skewers hot, garnished with fresh parsley or dill, if desired. Squeeze fresh lemon juice over the skewers just before serving.
Mediterranean Salmon Skewers are a delicious and healthy option for a summer barbecue or a light dinner. The combination of tender and flavorful salmon with the vibrant vegetables and Mediterranean seasonings creates a delightful meal. Serve them with a side of rice, couscous, or a fresh salad for a complete and satisfying dish. Enjoy!

Eggplant Steak Frites with Chimichurri

Ingredients:

For the Eggplant Steak:

2 large eggplants
1/4 cup olive oil
2 tablespoons balsamic vinegar
2 cloves garlic, minced
1 teaspoon smoked paprika
Salt and pepper, to taste

For the Frites (French Fries):

4 large russet potatoes
Vegetable oil, for frying
Salt, to taste

For the Chimichurri Sauce:

1 cup fresh parsley leaves, finely chopped
1/4 cup fresh cilantro leaves, finely chopped
3 cloves garlic, minced
2 tablespoons red wine vinegar
1/4 cup olive oil
1/2 teaspoon red pepper flakes (optional)
Salt and pepper, to taste

Instructions:

Preheat your grill to medium-high heat.
Slice the eggplants into thick rounds, about 1-inch thick.
In a bowl, whisk together the olive oil, balsamic vinegar, minced garlic, smoked paprika, salt, and pepper. Place the eggplant slices in a shallow dish and brush both sides generously with the marinade mixture. Let them marinate for about 15 minutes.
While the eggplant is marinating, prepare the Chimichurri sauce. In a small bowl, combine the chopped parsley, cilantro, minced garlic, red wine vinegar, olive oil, red pepper flakes (if using), salt, and pepper. Stir well to combine. Set aside to let the flavors meld.
Cut the russet potatoes into thin strips to make French fries. Rinse them in cold water to remove excess starch. Pat them dry with a clean kitchen towel or paper towels.
Heat vegetable oil in a deep fryer or a large pot to about 375°F (190°C). Fry the potatoes in batches until golden brown and crispy, about 4-5 minutes per batch. Remove them from the oil using a slotted spoon and transfer them to a paper towel-lined plate. Sprinkle with salt while still hot. Set aside.
Grill the marinated eggplant slices on the preheated grill for about 4-5 minutes per side, or until they are tender and have grill marks.
Remove the eggplant slices from the grill and let them cool slightly.
Serve the Eggplant Steak Frites by arranging the grilled eggplant slices on a plate, along with a generous serving of the crispy French fries. Drizzle the Chimichurri sauce over the eggplant steaks and serve any extra sauce on the side.
Eggplant Steak Frites with Chimichurri is a flavorful and satisfying vegetarian dish. The grilled eggplant slices provide a meaty texture, while the crispy French fries and zesty Chimichurri sauce complete the dish with a burst of freshness. Enjoy this delicious and hearty meal!

Campfire Caprese Brie

Ingredients:

1 wheel of Brie cheese
1 cup cherry tomatoes, halved
1/2 cup fresh basil leaves
2 tablespoons balsamic glaze
Salt and pepper, to taste
French baguette or crackers,
for serving

Instructions:

Prepare a campfire and let it burn down until you have a bed of hot coals.
Wrap the Brie cheese wheel in a double layer of heavy-duty aluminum foil, making sure it is fully enclosed. This will help protect the cheese from direct heat.
Place the foil-wrapped Brie on a grill grate or directly on the hot coals, ensuring it is not in direct contact with the flames. Cook for about 5-7 minutes, or until the cheese is soft and melty.
Carefully remove the foil-wrapped Brie from the campfire using tongs or heat-resistant gloves. Place it on a heatproof surface and let it cool slightly.
Unwrap the Brie and transfer it to a serving platter or a plate.
Arrange the cherry tomato halves and fresh basil leaves on top of the Brie.
Drizzle the balsamic glaze over the tomatoes and basil. Sprinkle with salt and pepper to taste.
Serve the Campfire Caprese Brie with slices of French baguette or crackers for dipping and spreading.
Campfire Caprese Brie is a delightful twist on the classic Caprese salad, with the addition of melted Brie cheese for a gooey and indulgent experience. The smoky flavors from the campfire add an extra dimension to this delicious appetizer. Enjoy it while still warm and gooey!

Grilled Creamed Corn

Ingredients:

4 ears of fresh corn, husked
2 tablespoons unsalted butter, melted
1/2 cup heavy cream
1/4 cup grated Parmesan cheese
1 tablespoon fresh chives, chopped
Salt and pepper, to taste

Instructions:

Preheat your grill to medium-high heat.
Brush the ears of corn with melted butter, making sure to coat them evenly.
Place the corn on the grill grates and cook for about 10-12 minutes, turning occasionally, until the corn is lightly charred and cooked through.
Remove the corn from the grill and let it cool slightly. Once cooled, stand each ear of corn upright on a cutting board and use a sharp knife to carefully cut the kernels off the cobs.
In a saucepan over medium heat, combine the corn kernels, heavy cream, grated Parmesan cheese, salt, and pepper. Stir well to combine.
Cook the mixture for about 5-7 minutes, stirring occasionally, until the cream has thickened and the corn is heated through.
Remove the pan from the heat and stir in the chopped chives.
Transfer the Grilled Creamed Corn to a serving dish or individual bowls.
Serve the Grilled Creamed Corn as a side dish or a topping for grilled meats. It's a rich and creamy twist on traditional corn on the cob, with the added smoky flavor from the grill.
Grilled Creamed Corn is a delicious and comforting dish that celebrates the natural sweetness of corn. The creamy sauce and charred kernels make it a perfect addition to your summer grilling menu. Enjoy!

Grilled Brussels Sprouts

Ingredients:

1 pound Brussels sprouts, trimmed and halved
2 tablespoons olive oil
2 cloves garlic, minced
1 teaspoon smoked paprika
Salt and pepper, to taste
Lemon wedges, for serving (optional)

Instructions:

Preheat your grill to medium-high heat.
In a large bowl, combine the Brussels sprouts, olive oil, minced garlic, smoked paprika, salt, and pepper. Toss well to coat the Brussels sprouts evenly with the seasonings.
Thread the Brussels sprouts onto skewers, placing them flat side down so they don't fall through the grill grates. If using wooden skewers, soak them in water for about 15 minutes beforehand to prevent them from burning.
Place the skewered Brussels sprouts on the preheated grill, directly over the heat. Close the lid and grill for about 8-10 minutes, turning occasionally, until the Brussels sprouts are lightly charred and tender.
Carefully remove the skewers from the grill and transfer the grilled Brussels sprouts to a serving platter.
Serve the Grilled Brussels Sprouts hot as a side dish. Squeeze fresh lemon juice over them just before serving, if desired, for a bright and tangy flavor.
Grilled Brussels Sprouts offer a delicious smoky flavor and caramelized edges, making them a delightful alternative to traditional boiled or roasted Brussels sprouts. They make a fantastic side dish for grilled meats or can be enjoyed on their own as a tasty and healthy snack. Enjoy!

I want to take a moment to express my heartfelt gratitude for your recent purchase of my recipe book. As a passionate food lover, nothing makes me happier than sharing my favorite recipes with others. Your decision to invest in my book not only supports my dream, but also shows your commitment to expanding your culinary horizons.

I sincerely hope that the recipes in the book will inspire you to try new things and add some excitement to your meals.

Thank you again for your support and for being a part of this journey with me. I hope my book will bring you many happy and delicious moments in the kitchen.

www.ingramcontent.com/pod-product-compliance
Lightning Source LLC
Chambersburg PA
CBHW081236080526
44587CB00022B/3956